STEM *trailblazer* BIOS

THEORETICAL
PHYSICIST
STEPHEN HAWKING

KARI CORNELL

Lerner Publications
Minneapolis

To Will. May you always have that extraordinary sense of wonder.

Lerner Publications Company
A division of Lerner Publishing Group, Inc.
241 First Avenue North
Minneapolis, MN 55401 USA

For reading levels and more information, look up this title at www.lernerbooks.com.

Content consultant: Liliya L. R. Williams, Professor, Minnesota Institute for Astrophysics

Library of Congress Cataloging-in-Publication Data

Cornell, Kari, author.
    Theoretical physicist Stephen Hawking / by Kari Cornell.
        pages cm. — (STEM trailblazer bios)
    Audience: Ages 7–11.
    Audience: Grades 4 to 6.
    Includes bibliographical references and index.
    ISBN 978-1-4677-9528-9 (lb : alk. paper) — ISBN 978-1-4677-9717-7 (pb : alk. paper) — ISBN 978-1-4677-9718-4 (eb pdf)
    1. Hawking, Stephen, 1942—Juvenile literature. 2. Physicists—Great Britain—Biography—Juvenile literature. 3. Amyotrophic lateral sclerosis—Patients—Great Britain—Biography. 4. Cosmology—Juvenile literature. I. Title. II. Series: STEM trailblazer bios.
    QC16.H33C67 2016
    530.092—dc23 [B]   2015021774

Manufactured in the United States of America
1 – BP – 12/31/15

The images in this book are used with the permission of: © iStockphoto.com/Adventure_Photo, p. 4; © Press Association/The Image Works, p. 5; Mary Evans Picture Library/Courtesy Everett Collection, p. 8; © Oxford Picture Library/Alamy, p. 11; © myLoupe//Universal Images Group/Getty Images, p. 12; Gillman & Soame UK Ltd, p. 14; © Spencer Sutton/Science Source, p. 15; © John Hedgecoe/TopFoto/The Image Works, p. 16; © Universal History Archive/UIG/Getty Images, p. 17; © Dorling Kindersley/Getty Images, p. 19; © Santi Visalli//Getty Images, p. 20; © David Gamble/TopFoto/The Image Works, p. 23; Ray Tang/Rex USA, p. 24; Local World/Rex USA, p. 25; Paramount/Courtesy Everett Collection, p. 26; © Focus Features/Courtesy Everett Collection, p. 27.

Front cover: © Mike Marsland/WireImage/Getty Images (main); NASA, ESA, and E. Sabbi/ESA/STScI (background).

Main body text set in Adrianna Regular 13/22. Typeface provided by Chank.

CONTENTS

Chapter 1

As a child, Stephen Hawking loved gazing at the night sky.

FASCINATED BY
THE STARS

On a warm summer evening in the early 1950s, young Stephen Hawking lay in the grass in front of his home in Saint Albans, England, and gazed up at the stars. His mother and his younger sisters were there too. As the damp grass tickled their toes, they took turns pointing out groupings of stars called constellations. Sometimes, they even saw falling stars.

Looking at the stars was one of Stephen's favorite things to do. But he also spent a lot of time thinking about stars. He wondered how the stars had come to be and if they would ever fade away. He didn't know it then, but he would spend his life searching for answers to these questions and many others. Stephen would become a **theoretical physicist**. That's a scientist who uses math to study ideas about how the universe began and how it might change in the future.

Hawking suffers from a motor neuron disease, but it has not slowed his efforts to learn about the universe.

EARLY YEARS

Stephen William Hawking was born in Oxford, England, on January 8, 1942. He likes to tell people that his birthday was exactly three hundred years after the death of Galileo, the famous Italian astronomer.

Stephen's father was a medical researcher who had gone to college at the University of Oxford. He studied tropical diseases. So he spent many months away from his family each year, doing research in Africa and other tropical places. He encouraged Stephen to study math and science. Someday, his father hoped, Stephen would become a medical doctor.

Stephen's mother went to college in Oxford during the 1930s, a time when most women didn't go to college. From

the time Stephen was very young, his mother could tell that he was bright. "Stephen always had a strong sense of wonder," she remembered. "And I could see that the stars would draw him."

Stephen was naturally curious about the stars and also about almost everything around him. He was especially interested in learning how things worked. Stephen often took apart clocks and radios to study how the parts inside fit together. When it came time to put the pieces back together, however, Stephen was stuck. His strength has always been in thinking things through, not in working with his hands.

TO SAINT ALBANS

In 1950, the Hawking family moved to Saint Albans, a small town 20 miles (32 kilometers) north of London, to be closer to Stephen's father's office. The Hawkings spent a lot of time reading, and they often ate dinner in silence, each with his or her nose in a book. The family also drove around town in an old taxicab, which Stephen's father had found for a cheap price after their old car broke down. Stephen was embarrassed to be seen in the cab, but his parents didn't really worry about what others thought.

Chapter 2

Stephen grew up in the 1950s in Saint Albans, England.

STUDYING MATH
AND PHYSICS

In 1953, Stephen attended St. Albans School. At eleven years old, Stephen was clever, but he didn't apply himself in school. In fact, during his first years, he ranked in the bottom half of his class. His many friends must have sensed that

Stephen was smart because they called him Einstein, after the famous physicist Albert Einstein.

Stephen's favorite teacher taught math, which quickly became the boy's favorite subject. However, Stephen's father discouraged his son from spending too much time studying math. He thought students who studied math could only become teachers, and he wanted Stephen to become a doctor. But becoming a doctor meant taking biology, and Stephen never liked biology. He liked chemistry, where experiments could lead to exciting and unexpected explosions. Stephen also did very well in **physics**, but he found it too easy to be interesting.

TECH TALK

"I had heard that light from distant galaxies was shifted . . . and that this was supposed to indicate that the universe was expanding. . . . But I was sure there must be some other reason. . . . An essentially unchanging and everlasting universe seemed so much more natural."

—*Stephen Hawking*

Outside of school, Stephen and his friends created complicated board games. Once, they used recycled parts to build a computer for solving basic math problems. In high school, the same group of friends held long talks about radio-controlled models, physics, and how the universe began. Stephen didn't believe the universe could be expanding, but some of his friends thought it might be. They discussed the different possibilities for hours.

OFF TO COLLEGE

When he was seventeen, Stephen took the entrance exam for college. His score had to be high enough to earn him a scholarship, money the university awards to students to pay for their schooling. Without a scholarship, Stephen's family could not afford to send him to college. He took the test in Oxford in March 1959.

Stephen remembered worrying about the results. "I was convinced I had done badly and was very depressed when, during the practical exam, university lecturers came around to talk to other students, but not to me," Stephen said. "Then, a few days after I got back from Oxford, I got a telegram to say I had received a scholarship."

Stephen had done very well. On the physics portion of the test, he earned a nearly perfect score. That fall, Stephen

Stephen received a scholarship to attend Oxford.

attended University College at Oxford, the same school as his father. Although Stephen really wanted to study math, the university didn't offer it as a major. Instead, he studied physics.

Again, Stephen didn't put much effort into his schooling. Yet, through his classes at University College, Stephen became more interested in **cosmology**, the study of how the universe formed. He graduated with a degree in natural science in 1962. Then Stephen decided to study cosmology at Trinity Hall at the University of Cambridge.

After he graduated from Oxford, Hawking studied cosmology at the University of Cambridge.

STUDYING THE UNIVERSE

As a graduate student at Cambridge, Hawking studied cosmology under Dennis Sciama. Although Hawking didn't always agree with Sciama's theories, their conversations did push Stephen to come up with his own ideas.

Hawking was determined to study cosmology and further explore Einstein's general theory of relativity. But few were studying cosmology at Cambridge at the time. So Hawking and a few other students took the train to London once a week to attend cosmology professor Hermann Bondi's lectures on relativity at King's College. Hawking also tracked down textbooks on relativity and studied them whenever he could.

THE GENERAL THEORY OF RELATIVITY

In 1915, Albert Einstein declared that time, distance, and speed are all relative. This means that each will vary depending on where you are, how you're moving, and how fast you're going. The only thing that always remains the same is the speed of light, or how fast light travels.

Chapter 3

During his schooling, Hawking took great interest in cosmology.

SHOCKING NEWS

In 1963, when Hawking was home for Christmas, he fell while ice-skating and couldn't stand up. Hawking had noticed that he was becoming clumsier. Sometimes, he tripped while

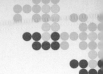

walking or fell down stairs. Hawking's mother took him to a doctor. After many tests, doctors finally discovered what was wrong. Hawking had amyotrophic lateral sclerosis (ALS). This disease eventually shuts down the nerves that control the muscles. Doctors told him that he had about two and a half years to live.

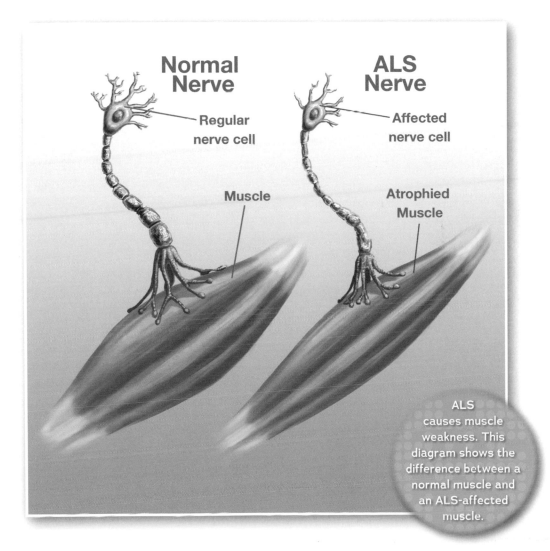

Normal Nerve

Regular nerve cell

Muscle

ALS Nerve

Affected nerve cell

Atrophied Muscle

ALS causes muscle weakness. This diagram shows the difference between a normal muscle and an ALS-affected muscle.

The news of Hawking's illness shocked him and his family. But it also inspired Hawking to make the most of what time he had left. He wanted to finish his PhD. He also wanted to spend time with Jane Wilde, a young woman he had just met at a New Year's Eve party. Completing his research and spending time with Wilde gave Hawking something to live for. He began to set goals and focused more on his work than he ever had before.

Hawking married Jane Wilde in 1965. Two of their children, Robert and Lucy, are shown here with them in 1978. Their third child, Timothy, was born the next year.

Black holes became a focal point for Hawking's research.

BLACK HOLES

Around this time, Hawking became interested in the research of a physicist named Roger Penrose, who studied **black holes**. Black holes are points in space that contain mass and have a very strong gravitational pull. Penrose proposed that black holes formed when dying stars collapsed in on themselves. Hawking thought this could be possible. He used Penrose's **theory** as a starting point for his own research about how the universe began.

Hawking thought a black hole might hold the answer to the question of how the universe was created. He reasoned that so many particles pushed together and bumping against one another would create energy. At some point, that energy must be released, so the particles expand or explode outward. This, he thought, might be what caused the **big bang**. This widely accepted theory suggests that the universe started out very small and quickly expanded.

TECH TALK

"My goal is simple. It is a complete understanding of the universe, why it is as it is, and why it exists at all."

—*Stephen Hawking*

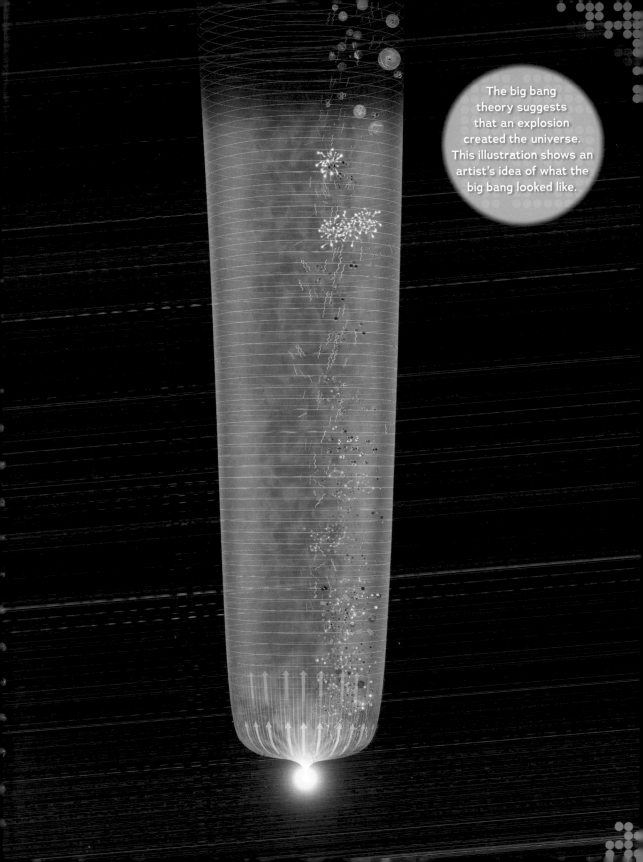

The big bang theory suggests that an explosion created the universe. This illustration shows an artist's idea of what the big bang looked like.

Chapter 4

In the 1970s, Hawking taught college classes in the United States and in England.

HONORS, OPPORTUNITIES, AND CHALLENGES

For the next decade, Hawking continued to study and think about black holes. In 1974, his research led to an important discovery: it's possible for **radiation** to escape the strong gravitational pull of black holes.

That same year, the Royal Society, the national academy of science in the United Kingdom, made Hawking a fellow, or an honored member. And Caltech in Pasadena, California, offered Hawking the chance to spend a year as a visiting professor of cosmology. The university was known for its strong physics research program.

The year in California was a success. Hawking returned to England with many new ideas. He began teaching classes at Gonville and Caius College at the University of Cambridge to support his wife Jane and their children while he continued to do research. In 1979, he was honored to learn that he had been named Lucasian Professor of Mathematics at Cambridge, a post once held by influential physicist Sir Isaac Newton.

BRUSH WITH DEATH

Throughout these successes, Hawking's health continued to worsen. By the mid-1970s, he was able to feed himself and get out of bed, but he needed help doing everything else. He used a wheelchair to get around. His speech had become so slurred that only those who knew him well could understand him. And the disease had begun to affect Hawking's breathing, causing him to have choking fits.

Hawking was on a research trip to Switzerland in 1985 when he came down with pneumonia. The illness nearly killed him. Jane insisted that they fly Hawking back to a hospital in Cambridge for care. The only way the doctors were able to save him was by giving him a tracheotomy. This procedure meant making a hole in his neck and throat and inserting a plastic tube through the hole to allow him to breathe. Although he could no longer speak, Hawking was still able to conduct research and do his work.

HAWKING'S COMPUTER

After the tracheotomy, a computer programmer in California designed a program that allowed Hawking to communicate. Hawking chose words on a laptop computer, and then a synthesizer turned the words into sounds. When Hawking lost the use of his hands, the program was adapted so that he could select words by moving his cheek across a computerized pad.

Hawking's computer allows him to communicate with others.

Chapter 5

A BRIEF HISTORY OF TIME
FROM THE BIG BANG TO BLACK HOLES

STEPHEN W. HAWKING
WITH AN INTRODUCTION BY CARL SAGAN

Hawking has written several books about the universe and how it began.

SCIENCE FOR EVERYONE

As a researcher, Hawking had written many papers and books about his findings. But he didn't write a book for a general audience until 1988, when he published *A Brief History of Time.* In the book, Hawking explained his discoveries and ideas about how the universe began, how he thought it might end, and everything in between. The book sold millions of copies and was translated into forty languages. Many people loved the book. But others claimed some of the explanations were still too difficult for nonscientists to understand. In response, Hawking wrote *The Universe in a Nutshell* in 2001. With pictures, graphics, and more basic descriptions, this book made cosmology much easier for the average reader to understand.

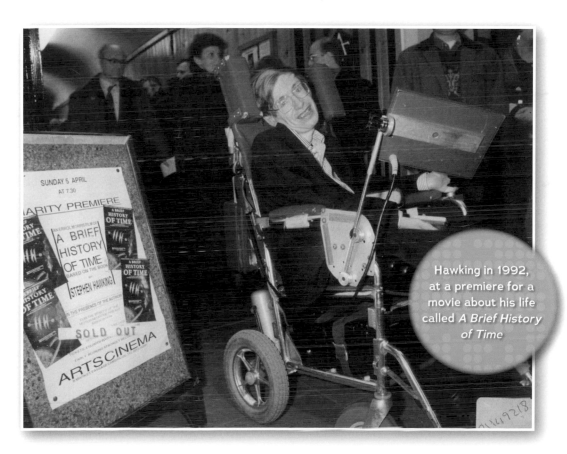

Hawking in 1992, at a premiere for a movie about his life called *A Brief History of Time*

The success of both books inspired Hawking to do more writing for general audiences. In 2007, Hawking and his daughter, Lucy, wrote a science adventure book for kids called *George's Secret Key to the Universe*. The first in a series of stories, this book explains difficult science concepts through an entertaining story line. Then, in 2010, Hawking published *The Grand Design*, in which he declared his belief that the universe was created through the big bang by physics alone, with no help from a creator.

Through his books and ideas, Hawking has become one of the most famous scientists of modern times. He's so famous that he's appeared on popular television shows such as *The Simpsons, The Big Bang Theory*, and *Star Trek: The Next Generation*. His life and his work have also been the subject of movies, including *The Theory of Everything*, which was released in 2014.

Hawking played himself in the television show *Star Trek: The Next Generation*.

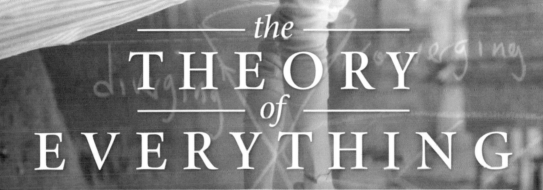

the
THEORY
of
EVERYTHING

The incredible story of Jane and Stephen Hawking

The Theory of Everything movie poster

His Mind Changed Our World.
Her Love Changed His.

FOCUS FEATURES PRESENTS A WORKING TITLE PRODUCTION EDDIE REDMAYNE FELICITY JONES
"THE THEORY OF EVERYTHING" CHARLIE COX EMILY WATSON SIMON McBURNEY WITH DAVID THEWLIS CASTING BY NINA GOLD
MUSIC BY JÓHANN JÓHANNSSON COSTUME DESIGNER STEVEN NOBLE HAIR MAKE-UP AND JAN SEWELL EDITOR JINX GODFREY PRODUCTION DESIGNER JOHN PAUL KELLY DIRECTOR OF PHOTOGRAPHY BENOÎT DELHOMME AFC
CO-PRODUCER RICHARD HEWITT EXECUTIVE PRODUCERS AMELIA GRANGER LIZA CHASIN DAVID KOSSE BASED ON THE BOOK "TRAVELLING TO INFINITY: MY LIFE WITH STEPHEN" BY JANE HAWKING
SCREENPLAY BY ANTHONY McCARTEN PRODUCED BY TIM BEVAN ERIC FELLNER LISA BRUCE ANTHONY McCARTEN DIRECTED BY JAMES MARSH FOCUS

STILL LOOKING FOR ANSWERS

Fifty years after Hawking was diagnosed with ALS and given a little more than two years to live, he still spends his days deep in thought about how the universe came to be. His ultimate goal is to come up with a single theory that explains how the universe began and how it will end, as well as everything that happened in between. To do this, Hawking has to consider what he's learned about the general theory of relativity. He also has to think about quantum mechanics, the science of how small particles of matter behave in space and time. Pulling together all of this knowledge is a big job, but if anyone can do it, Hawking can. He has the rare ability to think about and make connections among many theories at once.

SPACE TRAVEL

As Hawking ponders the beginning of the universe, he has become more interested in space travel. In 2007, he took a zero-gravity flight—a flight in which passengers experience what it's like to be in a space without gravity—over the Atlantic Ocean in a Boeing 727 airplane. Hawking loved it so much that he's already booked a flight on Virgin Atlantic's first planned commercial flight to space.

TIMELINE

1942

Stephen William Hawking is born in Oxford, England, on January 8.

1959

He takes the entry exam for University College at Oxford University. He earns a nearly perfect score on the physics portion and is awarded a scholarship.

1962

He graduates with honors with a degree in natural science and enrolls at Trinity Hall in Cambridge as a graduate student in cosmology.

1963

He is diagnosed with amyotrophic lateral sclerosis (ALS) at the age of twenty-one and begins to study black holes.

1974

He discovers that radiation can escape the gravitational pull of black holes, and the publication of his findings makes him a celebrity in the scientific world. He teaches at Caltech in California for a year.

1979

He becomes Lucasian Professor of Mathematics at Cambridge, a post once held by Sir Isaac Newton.

1985

He catches pneumonia and has a tracheotomy. He needs twenty-four-hour care and learns to talk through a computer.

1988

He publishes *A Brief History of Time*, a book explaining his cosmology findings to a general audience.

2001

He publishes *The Universe in a Nutshell*, a book that breaks down his findings into even more basic terms with illustrations.

2010

He publishes *The Grand Design*, in which he declares his belief that the universe was created by the big bang, not a creator.

SOURCE NOTES

6   Geoffrey Lean, "Prophet of Doomsday: Stephen Hawking, Eco-Warrior," Independent (London), January 21, 2007, http://www.independent.co.uk/environment/climate-change/prophet-of-doomsday-stephen-hawking-ecowarrior-433064.html.

7   Stephen Hawking," *Bio*, accessed May 18, 2015, http://www.biography.com/people/stephen-hawking-9331710.

9   Stephen Hawking, *My Brief History* (New York: Bantam, 2013), 26.

10 Ibid. 31–32.

18 John Boslough, *Stephen Hawking's Universe* (New York: William Morrow, 1985), 77.

GLOSSARY

big bang
the theory that the universe began with a huge explosion of space itself

black holes
points in space where gravity pulls everything nearby, including light, into them

cosmology
the science that studies the universe's structure, how the universe began, and how it changes

gravity
a force that pulls objects toward one another

physics
the science that studies matter and how it moves through space and time

radiation
a type of energy that travels through space

theoretical physicist
a scientist who uses math and physics to explain or predict why things happen

theory
a statement that explains how or why something happens

FURTHER
INFORMATION

BOOKS

Hawking, Lucy, and Stephen Hawking. *George's Secret Key to the Universe*. New York: Simon & Schuster, 2007. Stephen Hawking wrote this fun adventure through space for kids with his daughter, Lucy.

Scott, Elaine. *Space, Stars, and the Beginning of Time: What the Hubble Telescope Saw*. New York: Clarion Books, 2011. Through the lens of the Hubble Telescope, readers learn how the universe evolved.

Zuchora-Walske, Christine. *Key Discoveries in Earth and Space Science*. Minneapolis: Lerner Publications, 2015. Learn about some of the important theories and discoveries that led to the current understanding of space.

WEBSITES

Black Holes: NASA Science Astrophysics
http://science.nasa.gov/astrophysics/focus-areas/black-holes
Learn more about black holes and the big bang.

Einstein's Theory of Relativity: *Space.com*
http://www.space.com/28738-einstein-theory-of-relativity
-explained-infgraphic.html
Explore a step-by-step history of relativity spelled out in words and pictures.

Stephen Hawking: The Official Website
http://www.hawking.org.uk
Read more about Stephen Hawking's life, books, and discoveries.

LERNER

Expand learning beyond the printed book. Download free, complementary educational resources for this book from our website, www.lerneresource.com.

SOURCE™

INDEX

ABOUT THE AUTHOR

Kari Cornell is a freelance writer and editor who lives with her husband, two sons, and dog in Minneapolis, Minnesota. One of her favorite things to do is to write about people who've found a way to do what they love. When she's not writing, she likes tinkering in the garden, cooking, and making something clever out of nothing. Learn more about her work at karicornell.wordpress.com.